Dear Parents and Educators,

Welcome to Penguin Young Readers! As parents and educators, you know that each child develops at his or her own pace—in terms of speech, critical thinking, and, of course, reading. Penguin Young Readers recognizes this fact. As a result, each Penguin Young Readers book is assigned a traditional easy-to-read level (1–4) as well as a Guided Reading Level (A–P). Both of these systems will help you choose the right book for your child. Please refer to the back of each book for specific leveling information. Penguin Young Readers features esteemed authors and illustrators, stories about favorite characters, fascinating nonfiction, and more!

Look! I Can Read!

LEVEL **2**

GUIDED
READING
LEVEL **F**

This book is perfect for a **Progressing Reader** who:
• can figure out unknown words by using picture and context clues;
• can recognize beginning, middle, and ending sounds;
• can make and confirm predictions about what will happen in the text; and
• can distinguish between fiction and nonfiction.

Here are some **activities** you can do during and after reading this book:
• Picture Clues: Picture clues help young readers figure out the meaning of words. Read this book and have the child point to the pictures and the corresponding words.
• Sight Words: Sight words are frequently used words that readers must know just by looking at them. These words are known instantly, on sight. Knowing these words helps children develop into efficient readers. The sight words listed below appear in this book. As you read the story, have the child point out the sight words.

can	here	it	of	stop	what
for	I	know	one	this	with
from	is	my	see	to	you

Remember, sharing the love of reading with a child is the best gift you can give!

—Bonnie Bader, EdM, and Katie Carella, EdM
  Penguin Young Readers program

*Penguin Young Readers are leveled by independent reviewers applying the standards developed by Irene Fountas and Gay Su Pinnell in *Matching Books to Readers: Using Leveled Books in Guided Reading*, Heinemann, 1999.

For Emily—SH

For Mark, who sometimes reads to me—AW

Penguin Young Readers
Published by the Penguin Group
Penguin Group (USA) Inc., 375 Hudson Street, New York, New York 10014, USA
Penguin Group (Canada), 90 Eglinton Avenue East, Suite 700,
Toronto, Ontario M4P 2Y3, Canada
(a division of Pearson Penguin Canada Inc.)
Penguin Books Ltd., 80 Strand, London WC2R 0RL, England
Penguin Group Ireland, 25 St. Stephen's Green, Dublin 2, Ireland (a division of Penguin Books Ltd.)
Penguin Group (Australia), 250 Camberwell Road, Camberwell, Victoria 3124, Australia
(a division of Pearson Australia Group Pty. Ltd.)
Penguin Books India Pvt. Ltd., 11 Community Centre, Panchsheel Park, New Delhi—110 017, India
Penguin Group (NZ), 67 Apollo Drive, Rosedale, Auckland 0632, New Zealand
(a division of Pearson New Zealand Ltd.)
Penguin Books (South Africa) (Pty.) Ltd., 24 Sturdee Avenue, Rosebank,
Johannesburg 2196, South Africa

Penguin Books Ltd., Registered Offices: 80 Strand, London WC2R 0RL, England

Library of Congress Control Number: 00-035354

ISBN 978-0-448-41967-1   11

Look! I Can Read!

by Susan Hood

illustrated by Amy Wummer

Penguin Young Readers
An Imprint of Penguin Group (USA) Inc.

I can read

"Milk."

I can read "Stop."

I can read "School."

I can read
"Shop."

I know my letters

from **A** to **Z**.

A is for ant.

B is for bee.

What starts with **C**?

Carrots and cheese.

Can you find something here

for each one of these?

Look at the picture and find an object
that begins with each letter from **D** to **Z**.

I wrote my name.

I'll read it to you.

Mommy, can **you** read this?

See? I love you!

My dad reads to me
at bedtime each night.

He shows me you read
from the left to the right.

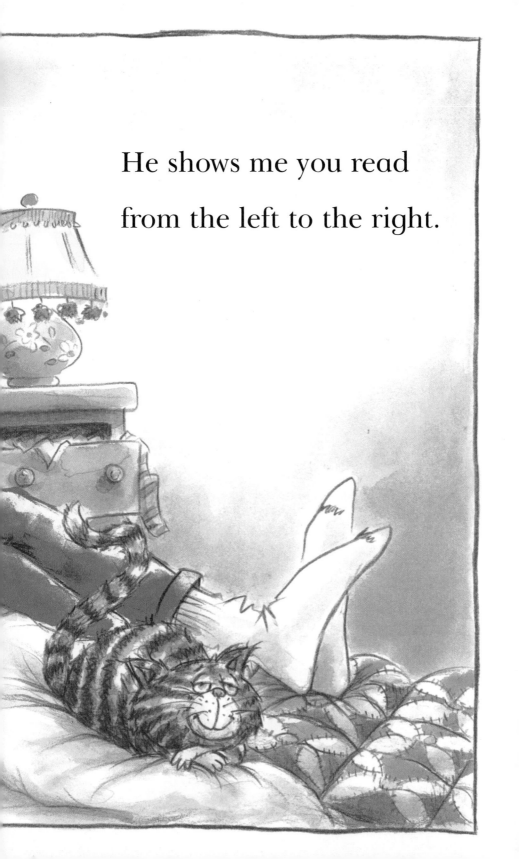

Now I read words
in the grocery store.

I can read words

in a tree . . .

. . . on the floor.

The pictures help me
as I read and I look.

30

Hey, Mommy,

guess what!

I read this
whole book!